My HEART *in* TIME

LIVING PROOF OF GOD'S CONTINUAL GRACE THROUGH LIFE'S CHALLENGES

DONNA WILKINSON MAXWELL

xulon
PRESS

My Heart in Time
Living proof of God's continual Grace through life's challenges
by Donna Wilkinson Maxwell

Printed in the United States of America

ISBN 9781628399738

www.xulonpress.com

DEDICATION

Live and declare the works of the Lord.
For René, Roman, Morgan and
generations yet unborn.

be encouraged

Ronnie Wilkinson Maxwell

THE PASSAGE OF TIME

At birth you were given a mysterious amount of it…
As a child you simply had enough of it…
As a youth, you enjoyed it without care for it…
You did not cherish it… Time.

As an adult you wonder, where is it…?
Going so fast, why can't it quit… Time.
As a senior you want to be done with it
It is taking too long… too long
This is it… Time.
Why can't I get rid of it… or just pass it on…

Some of my friends call me dramatic. I really could not understand why. It bothered me to such a degree that I was inspired to write:

DRAMA QUEEN

They say I'm a "Drama Queen."
They say I'm high strung.
But what do they know of me,
And the things that I've done?
Because I feel deeply,
And maybe a bit verbose,
Because I'm more vocal than most?

What does a "Drama Queen" do anyway?
Why are they making note of everything I say?
They must think a lot of me to put a label, agree?
"Drama Queen," I can't believe it!
Oh, what a mess!
If they'd say Diva, then I'd agree,
YES!

Journey is about change, transition and simply moving on.

JOURNEY

The end of an era, the end of an age
To face new challenges as I turn a new page
In this book called "My story"
Some pages tear stained and some filled with glory.
I will reflect on the faces from the years gone by
Indelibly imprinted on the pages of my life…
Friendships forged through our daily grind
Lives brought together and forever entwined.

Though parting is bitter sweet,
My leaving is not surrender or defeat.
In life's journey we must go on,
To face our destiny, we are not yet done.
The good times we have shared and there
were many of those,
I will cherish the memories and hold them close.
Having you in my life has made it greater,
Thank God it is not goodbye, but see you later…

Just thinking about life:

CONTEMPLATION

Sitting, steering into space
Wondering what I'm doing in this place
Life is going on and I do not have a plan
What can I do? I do not understand
But with the passing of time in this life sublime
What can I do to make it mine?
I think about the times gone by
Wasted years I could have applied
Myself to the task of doing something memorable
Without wasting time around life's table,
How can I improve myself and do much better?
I can get up from this table
Do something greater
I know… I am able.
Awake from your stupor with a new attitude
Push ahead with great fortitude
Don't look back at life's aberration
For it was only a temporary deviation
Look ahead with expectation
Courage, enthusiasm, confidence
These are the words we will use that brings promise
Anticipation, elation, happiness and hope
These are the words that will allow you to cope.

HAPPINESS

Where does it come from?
Is it from you or is it from me?
Can I buy it or is it free?
Can I touch it, does it see?
Will it stay around or will it flee?
Where is happiness?
Can someone please tell me,
Why is it being illusive?

Did someone hide it?
Is it invisible?
I've looked all around
This is absolutely incredible!

Stop, wait… something is stirring
I think I feel it!
Buried deep inside
I don't have to buy it!
I don't have to borrow it!
It is free… deep inside of me.
So wake up happiness, exercise your bone,
Stretch your muscles, flex, extend,
Make yourself known.
Don't hide… there is nothing to be afraid of
Make yourself known,
After all, you're grown!

My marriage:

IMPERFECTLY PERFECT

You have not been the perfect husband…
And I have not been the perfect wife
But through our imperfect lives
God's Grace and Mercy has shown bright.
We have learned some difficult lessons
Things have not always gone our way
At times happiness evaded and we wanted to run away
But we have hung in through the challenges
And remembered the promises we made to each other
Of love and respect for one another
So when faced with hard choices and temptations sweet
We'll feel the heart that beats beneath our breast
And the day we vowed to each other and said, yes.
With our eyes on the future of innocence and promise
Days untarnished in which to exist
Help us to celebrate this gift from above
As we embrace our imperfectly perfect love.

Courage was written for two of my dear friends who have chosen to honor God with their lives.

COURAGE

Courage in the face of adversity,
This is what your life has taught me.
Courage to make difficult decisions
Trusting God to make provisions.
With your life built on Almighty God
Courage is sometimes all you had.
Courage is a life shining bright,
The evidence of God's eternal light.
As the moon reflects the sun
Your life reflects "The Holy One"
With faith in God your courage builds
For life's journey through valleys and hills.
So continue on courageous ones;
Fight for the battle is not yet done.
As warriors lift your banners high;
Raise it with honor to the sky,
For when the journey is done and the battle won,
God will say, "thou good and faithful daughter and son."

This was written for my beloved daughter, René. René in turn handed it down to her daughter, Morgan. We trust that Morgan will in time, hand this poem to her daughter and so on, for generations to come. It is my prayer that you will share this with your daughter as well.

MOTHER TO DAUGHTER

Daughter of my heart,
May God hold you apart…
From the rest;
Close to His breast
Enclose you in His love and
Encompass you with angels from above.
Daughter of my heart
May you always…start your day with God the head of all
Your desires;
Your hopes;
Your dreams;
Life's fleeting and changing scenes.
Daughter of my heart, I love you!

The next few poems were written during my mom's final days and some completed after her passing. I wanted to capture her essence. I wanted her to know how much she meant to me and the impression her life left on all those she came in contact with.

Tribute to Mother

THE STAR THAT LIGHTS OUR WAY, DARLING MOTHER DEAR

Darling Mother ever near
You always had a song to share
You said it would drive away the fear
A song in the heart, a song on the lips.
Oh, how my heart still skips a beat
When I recall your voice with that melody so sweet.

You gave your love continuously,
You gave your love sincerely.
Your face always shone with the countenance of the Son
Your smile would light the world,
"Oh, what a beautiful lady", I often heard.

Your light has not gone out, as some would say,
Your light continues to shine every day

It shines in your children, grandchildren

13

and generations on the way.
So shine on my mother in glory land,
Shine on my mother for we will stand.
Stand for the life you taught us,
Shine for the joy you brought us,
A life of integrity and prayer
Through hardship and care
You never gave up the fight,
You never gave up the light.

Shine on, Darling Mother!
You are a bright shining star in heaven now!

GOD'S WARRIOR

You fought long and you fought hard
You never gave up
You fought with prayer, the Word and a song
You fought hard and you fought long.
The word of God your shield and protection
You marched on with purpose and direction
You fought hard and you fought long
And now the battle is won.

WILL YOU CARRY ON?

I did my best, you may not understand.
I did my best, it may not have been grand.
I did my best to instill in you all
The things that God taught me
The joy and pain it brought me
I carried the mantle the torch of the Lord
So don't be discouraged
Don't cry for too long
Just answer the question: Will you carry on?

KEEP A SONG IN YOUR HEART

When you are down, keep a song in your heart;
When you feel discouraged, keep a song on your lips;
When you are distressed, give praise to the Lord,
He will bring joy what'er the discord.
He will keep you through; just give it to Him,
You will be encouraged when you hum a hymn.

YOU CAN COUNT ON ME

Count on me when you are helpless;
Count on me to see you through;
Count on me when you need a shoulder to lean on,
Count on me when you are feeling blue.
I did it all because I was able to count on you!

PEACE PERFECT

God loves perfect peace
Mama taught me these words at least;
When I was little and sat on her knees
She said, Don what does God love?
And she would answer...God loves perfect peace.
I was quite little and didn't understand the text.
She asked: Don, what does God love,
I said, "Peace Perfect".

BORN OF A "MOTHER DEAR"

I was born of a mother dear, a mother fair

A mother who cared to share all, no matter what the call

Buyer

Seller

Sewer

Machine operator

Housekeeper

Yard sale for flea market sales

She did it all…

Mother Dear, Mother Fair,

You showed us the way; yes, the truth and the life.

Your prayer was for us to do right

To stay on the straight and narrow

To lend and not borrow

To pray and seek peace

To work for the Lord and not to be at ease

Mother Dear, Mother Fair

Woman of God, I love you.

Knowing just how much God loves us, we cannot afford the mistake of ignoring Him.

THE CALLING

I wake up, I go on my way
I struggle through every day
Do I take the time to pray?
Do I take the time to say:
'Lord, please take me through another day"
I just go on my way.

I hear a small still voice. I make a choice, no… not today
I just go on my way.

Do I even stop to listen?
I pretend I do not hear
Or even thank God for his blessin'
It seems as if I do not care.

Should I care that Jesus loves me, died for me,
watches over me?
Should I care that the Son of God left his home above,
Just because of love?
Should I care that He knows my hurts,
the longing in my soul,

Loves me enough to make me whole?
To take me to his home above, just because of love?
I pretend I do not hear... I do not care.

But how long?
Can I ignore a love so true, so pure, so perfect,
That draws me to become His child, His elect?
Can I ignore a love that died on Calvary,
Whose sole purpose on this earth is to become joy,
happiness and peace, all for me?
Can I ignore a love that's preparing a place
to save me from sin and disgrace?
NO!
I can hold out no longer!
My soul is longing for you, a love so pure,
so perfect, so true.
Forgive me Lord for my sin
As you prepare a place, please let me in.
Forgive me Lord if I've ignored
A love that endured
All for me, just to set me free.

Inspired by the Holy Spirit:

RAIN

I see the rain, the drops scatter and then flow and come
together as one.
I see the rain and I wonder why it flows,
Then I know – without it we will not grow.
So let it rain.
Lord, let it flow for us to grow and cleanse our soul.
Rain your Holy Spirit and we will get together as one.

I hear the rain and I feel comfort.
There is a peace in my soul
Because I know the Holy Spirit will cleanse me.
Sweet rain, blessed rain – I need your cleansing
Only you can bring.
I feel freedom in my soul.
Sweet peace,
Sweet freedom,
Sweet cleansing,
Sweet rain.

Growing up in Portland, Jamaica, I saw my parents struggle to make ends meet for their family. They had one essential piece of survival tool, love.

MOM AND DADDY

We lived in the country when I was small
With mom taking care of us all
We had it hard there was no doubt
But mom was a hard worker;
she knew what love was about.

Daddy would come from Kingston on weekend, you see
He would bring us some food
So we wouldn't go hungry.
As children we waited for daddy by the gate
We looked for him in the distance and
hoped he'd not be late.
Mom and daddy did all that they could
To take care of their family as they felt they should.

I get tears in my eyes when I think of those days
Although long gone, I'll miss them always.
Life was hard there's no doubt
But mom and daddy knew what love was about.

MY DADDY

He was a tradesman with saw and hammer in his hand.
Worked hard all his life
To make things better for children and wife.
He'd always say, "I've worked in every Parish in Jamaica
Building houses
Churches
And maybe even for the "undertaker."
Daddy was hospitable
Loved having visitors at his table.
He would tell many stories
Of all his conquests and former glories.
He loved to play domino
He'd always win, don't you know
My daddy was a great man,
Always did his best
With saw and hammer in his hand,
He passed the test!

Questions of life, I am still trying to understand.

LOVE...?

What is love?
Can you touch it, see it or feel it with your heart
Does love care for you
Protect you
Provide for you
Or does love just, speak?
Does love put into action what it says?
Or does love just lay there...dead.

Does love leave you without a thought?
Does love come back, or is it brought?
Can you touch it, see it or feel it with your heart?
Does love understand that it has a part?

LIFE'S DISAPPOINTMENTS

What do you do when your dreams are shattered?
Your aspirations battered and bruised?
Do you just give up when the task seems great
And it would seem you have all to lose?
Do you hang your head down low and sigh
Or do you feel you'll just give up and cry.
Well, maybe for a little while, you realize self-pity is an isle.
You are on your own, you feel so alone…

After a while you think there must be
a solution to this problem.
You can't go on in this direction
This is nothing but self-destruction
So you lift your head up high
You dry your tears, you no longer cry.
You take a breath and say
This is a new day there must be a better way
You take another breath
And you realize this is life not death.
So live you best life now
You'll find that how you handle life's disappointments
Will teach you how to cherish its greatest moments.

Written for one of my dearest friends, he is the caregiver for his brother who is diagnosed with a mental disorder. The love for his brother is demonstrated in his dedication to ensure that he is not just another statistic. Kudos to you!

DIFFERENT

For as long as I can remember
I knew you were different.
As children growing up, you were just so distant.
There was a problem we could not understand
But it seemed much greater
Certainly not what we had planned
But there was no other, my blood…my brother.

Then different became belligerent
We did not know what to do
It must be a discipline problem,
that's what they said at school.
This was more than we could manage
We had no idea how to build
That bridge and stop all the damage
But still there was no other, my blood…my brother.

You grew up and left home
You took to the streets and there you roam.

We couldn't help you, we only faced defeat.
So we left you to walk the beat.
Your actions were not intentional,
You just needed some help,
You were actually institutional.
You couldn't do it by yourself.
Still yet there was no other, by blood…my brother.

Although it is difficult and certainly not grand,
I've taken you under my roof to lend a helping hand.
You can take comfort that I'll do my best,
So you can have shelter, peace and rest.
At times I'll need to rejuvenate,
Regain my strength so I can relate,
Have a clear mind to handle the task
Which I do freely, you don't have to ask.
With confidence I can say,
There is no other, my blood…my brother.

This poem was written at the request of my daughter René. She asked me to attend a group home to speak to young girls who were pregnant or already had a child. I wanted them to know that there is hope. Even when you cannot see your way, you can hold your head up high. You have a future.

<u>WHEN I TURN 18</u>

Growing up I couldn't wait to be eighteen years old.
I just wanted to party and not do as I was told.
I dreamt about being eighteen to do as I would,
Going to parties and just up to no good.
I was a very good student you see
Inducted into the National Honor Society
But that was not as important to me
I wanted to be eighteen, so I could "party."

My elaborate plan was not to be
For when I turned eighteen, I had a baby.
Nine days before my eighteenth birthday
I gave birth to a baby, named René.
I was too young to be a mother
But when my baby was born, I would have no other.
My priority had to change I could party no longer
For my baby needed me to be her mother.

I received the skills to obtain a job to feed my baby
There was no time for me to be lazy.
I wanted the best for her that was sure,
I loved my baby girl, her heart I adore.

So now when I look at "my baby girl, René"
I see how God has blessed us all along the way.
God gave me a proper child
Who has grown into a Godly woman
and a loving mother so mild.

When I was young, it was hard for me to imagine that one day "I'd" be fifty! How absurd but here it is! It is a big number, but I am so thankful to see this day. Time is moving on…it does not stand still.

FIFTY

Fifty, over the hill
Can't find a thrill
Things slowing down,
Putting on the pounds.
Cholesterol, diabetes, blood pressure
Must keep then all in check
Oh, what a pain in the neck!

Fifty, is this how things will go down?
Now I understand the "gravity" of the situation all around.
What is that heat?
Having a personal summer in the middle of winter!
Oh my back hurts and my knees are cracking
and it just won't stop
And try as I might, oh what a sight,
I can only "drop it" like it's "not."
Fellows you are not off the hook
You must check your prostate
And please don't be late or disappointment may be your fate.

Fifty, you know what?

It doesn't have to be as some portray it, you see.

I will take care of me.

Keep it moving: exercise, take my vitamins

Yes, I can still and will be happy.

Fifty and free: I can travel on land or sea

Concentrate on me.

Fifty, time to reflect and correct all that I did wrong

And those I treated with neglect.

Fifty and free, children gone and the nest is empty.

Fifty and free, time to take care of me.

In memory of my sister Carol and in honor of her girls: Dione, Judith and Monique.

ROSES FOR MY SISTER

Those days when life was easy
Doing those things that pleased me
I knew my sister had my back
Praying for me not to go down "that track."
My sister was a Christian
She had confidence and assurance that God can
Do anything He chose to do
Even save her little sister she knew
He would come through.
Even when I went the wrong way
With prayer and a song she continued to say…
Sister chose the right path,
For only the good will last.
But as time went on and all things change under the sun,
We grew apart this sister of my heart.
She is gone now to take her rest
But she has left behind her "best"
Three Roses that have blossomed
Under tender care in her bosom
They'll carry the memory of her love,
These beautiful Roses from above.

Written for the Ladies of Rehoboth:

THE HAT PARADE

Ladies marching in the Hat Parade
Looking so beautiful as they promenade
Showing versatility with hats galore
Pardon me… sand back
And let me hold the door.
Hats of great prominence
Hats that show dominance
Hats that are demure
Those are the ones I love and adore.

Truly significant is this Hat Parade
As the ladies dexterity is displayed
How many hats do you have, I wonder?
Well, let me tell you a story and you can ponder.

It's not just the physical hat that you see
These hats signify our life's story:

Single lady… free, independent and happy
Wearing her hat… oh yes, she is sassy
Looking ahead at life: the possibilities and probabilities
I wonder what they'll be, I cannot wait to see.

The hat of a mother and a father, if needed
The hat of the bread winner pushing forward unimpeded
Doing what's necessary to survive
Making ends meet, take a breath, keep moving
Thank God, I am alive.

My hat now may be tattered and torn
Telling the tale of a life some paths forlorn
But when I look at this battered hat
I see years gone by, secrets kept, smiles, tears…
Laughter and all that.
So I am not saddened by my hat well worn
I do not dwell on the dreams unborn
I just smile and think, what a life I've had
As I gaze at my tattered and torn hat.

Yes, a significant part of this Hat Parade:
Pardon me, stand back as we promenade.

A FLEETING FRIEND

I try to hold on to you

But you just keep slipping away.

You hate being held

But you want to be cherished

How can I love you when you constantly run away from me?

I want to get enough of you,

But you will not be confined or be taken advantage of.

You are so precious to me

I will try to be wise in how I spend

And be careful not to waste

Any more of your…

TIME

www.donnawilkinsonmaxwell.com

CPSIA information can be obtained at www.ICGtesting.com
Printed in the USA
BVOW06s0136071113

335678BV00005B/10/P